SCOOBY-DOO!
SPACE DISCOVERIES

SPOTTING STARS AND CONSTELLATIONS WITH VELMA

by Ailynn Collins

CAPSTONE PRESS
a capstone imprint

Published by Capstone Press, an imprint of Capstone
1710 Roe Crest Drive
North Mankato, Minnesota 56003
capstonepub.com

Library of Congress Cataloging-in-Publication Data
is available on the Library of Congress website.

ISBN: 9781669021261 (hardcover)
ISBN: 9781669021162 (paperback)
ISBN: 9781669021223 (ebook PDF)

Summary: Come along with science expert Velma and other members of
the Mystery Inc. gang, and learn what constellations you can spot, how
stars form, and how stars can die in huge explosions. Under Velma's
magnifying glass, you'll get a close-up look at stars like never before!

Editorial Credits
Editor: Carrie Sheely; Designer: Elyse White;
Media Researcher: Rebekah Hubstenberger;
Production Specialist: Whitney Schaefer

Image and Design Credits
Alamy: Matteo Omied, 11 (middle right); Getty Images: Hulton Archive, 9
(bottom right), MARK GARLICK, 6-7, MARK GARLICK/SCIENCE PHOTO
LIBRARY, front cover (middle right); NASA: The Hubble Heritage Team
(AURA/STScI), 8-9, JSC/Serena Auñón-Chancellor, 28; Science Source:
ALMA (ESO/NAOJ/NRAO)/Alexandra Angelich (NRAO/AUI/NSF), 13,
ALMA/ESO, 21 (top), Chris Butler, 25 (bottom left), John Chumack, front
cover (top left); Shutterstock: Aphelleon, back cover (background), 1, 32,
Art Furnace, 14-15 (background), cddesign.co, design element (planets),
dore art, 22 (middle right), Forgem, 18-19 (background), GoodStudio,
4 (telescope), Imageman, 26-27, Iron Mary, front cover (bottom right),
Jazziel, 15 (constellation), 16-17, 24 (constellation), 24-25 (background),
Marc Ward, 21 (bottom left), 23 (constellation), MichaelTaylor, 10-11,
OHishiapply, 22-23 (background), Pike-28, front cover (background),
2-3, 30-31, seveniwe, 5 (middle right), Vector FX, 18 (constellation),
Vitalii Bashkatov, 4-5 (background)

Table of Contents

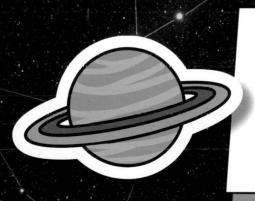

Words in **bold** are in the glossary.

Stars, Constellations, and Asterisms

Stars blanket the night sky with twinkling light. Long ago, people looked up at the stars just like we do now. They joined the points of stars together and imagined seeing shapes of animals or characters from well-known stories.

Groovy! I can see the Big Dipper! Scoob, I'd be able to scoop you a lot of Scooby snacks with a spoon that big!

Scooby snacks? Yum!

The Big Dipper is just one of the star groupings in our night sky. It's part of a big constellation called Ursa Major.

The seven bright stars of the Big Dipper make the asterism easy to spot.

Today, scientists group these imagined shapes into constellations and asterisms. A constellation is a large area of space where the stars make a pattern or outline. Sometimes smaller patterns made of fewer stars are inside constellations. These are called asterisms.

The Big Dipper is probably the most well-known asterism in North America. It's made of seven stars, and it looks like a giant soup ladle or scoop.

Chapter 1

Stars are Born and Stars Die

Stars are giant balls of gas that give off light and heat. These gases are mostly hydrogen and helium. Scientist Cecilia Payne-Gaposchkin discovered that stars were made of these gases in 1925. Before then, scientists believed the sun and Earth were made of the same **elements**.

One way **astronomers** group stars is by their temperature. They put stars in groups from coolest to hottest.

Did you know that the closest star to us is our very own sun? That's right! Our sun is a star.

Blue stars tend to shine the brightest in the night sky. They blast out much more energy than Earth's sun.

A star's color tells us how hot or cold it is. Blue stars are the hottest. Their surface temperatures can be between 10,000 and 50,000 kelvin (K) (17,540 and 89,540 degrees Fahrenheit).

Red stars are the coolest. Even these cool stars are very hot. They can have temperatures of about 3,500 K (5,840°F).

In between blue and red stars are white, yellow, and orange stars. Our sun is a yellow star. Its surface temperature is about 6,000 K (10,340°F).

Star Colors and Temperatures

Color	Example	Surface Temperature (K)
Blue	Rigel	10,000-50,000
White	Vega	7,500-10,000
Yellow	Earth's sun	5,000-6,000
Orange	Alpha Centauri B	3,500-5,000
Red	Antares	2,500-3,500

A halo of light called a light echo surrounds a red supergiant star, showing a dust cloud.

Astronomers also group stars by their **mass**. Stars can be dwarfs, giants, or supergiants.

Red dwarfs are the most common. They're about half the mass of our sun. They live for a long time because they burn slowly. They can live trillions of years.

Yellow dwarfs are medium-sized stars that live at least 10 billion years. Our sun is a yellow dwarf star. It's middle-aged. Scientists think it has about 5 billion years of energy left to burn.

Giant stars can be as big as 100 times the size of our sun. They don't appear to be that big because they're so far away.

Supergiant stars are even bigger. They can be more than 1,500 times the size of our sun. Some supergiant stars live for about 300,000 years. Others may live as long as 50 million years.

Our sun has more mass than all the **planets** orbiting it combined. It's most closely packed, or dense, at the core.

Not as dense as my s'more is going to be! Pile on the chocolate, Scoob!

FACT
In the early 1900s, astronomer Annie Jump Cannon helped develop the Harvard spectral classification system. It is a way scientists classify stars today.

Artwork of dust and gases swirling around a protostar

Stars are born in space clouds. Space is full of dust and gas that form enormous clouds called nebulae. The gases in the nebulae are mostly hydrogen and helium. The dust and gases swirl around. Their own **gravity** then pulls everything together into a clump.

The clump begins to spin faster. Everything becomes tightly packed into the middle. It gets smaller and rounder. Eventually, it forms into a ball shape. This is called a protostar.

As the protostar forms, it also gets hotter. When the temperature gets to 1.8 million°F (1 million°C), hydrogen gas **atoms** fuse together to become helium. This happens in a process called **nuclear fusion**.

Fusion releases a lot of energy that keeps the middle of the star hot. In this way, a new star is born.

The Orion Star Nursery

Stargazers enjoy looking at the Orion Nebula inside the Orion constellation. The nebula is easily seen from Earth with a telescope. This cloud is a big star-forming region, or stellar nursery. It has around 1,000 young stars. Four hot, large stars in the center of the Orion Nebula make up the Trapezium.

Orion Nebula

The Orion Nebula is one of the most studied and photographed objects in our night sky!

Now that's some star power!

A star's death can take billions of years. The more massive a star is, the faster it burns through the hydrogen in its core. The outer layers expand, and the star becomes a red giant. The star sheds its outer layers. Eventually, fuel runs out, and the core cools. The star slowly fades away and dies.

A supergiant star burns through its fuel fast. It dies with a huge explosion. This is called a **supernova**. The supernova is the biggest type of explosion in the sky.

Scientists think a supernova can leave behind a black hole. A black hole is a place in space where gravity is the strongest.

A black hole has so much gravity that nothing can escape it, not even light.

Zoinks! Like, let's never travel to a black hole, Scoob! We'll never escape!

Reah!

Artwork of Supernova 1987A shows pieces of the exploded star in red. The outer white and blue coloring shows where the blast wave is colliding with gas.

Chapter 2

Stars in the Spotlight

The night sky looks different depending on where you are on Earth. Some stars are better seen in the Southern **Hemisphere**. Others are clearer in the Northern Hemisphere. Some stars can be seen only from one hemisphere.

Pollux and Castor are two stars that appear close together in the sky. They are in the Gemini constellation. In the Northern Hemisphere, stargazers can draw a line diagonally from the handle of the Big Dipper to the other corner of the scoop. If they follow that line farther north, they'll see these very bright twin stars. Castor is not just one star, but six stars close together.

Pollux is closer to Earth, about 34 light-years away. One light-year is 5.88 trillion miles (9.46 trillion km). Castor is 51 light-years away.

Castor

Pollux

FACT
Stars don't stay still. They spin, and they zoom around the **galaxy**. Even dead stars go on spinning.

Like, all that spinning would make me dizzy!

It sure would! The fastest known spinning star in our universe rotates once every 25 seconds!

After our sun, the next brightest star in our night sky is Sirius. It is in the Canis Major, or the Greater Dog, constellation. Sirius is also called the Dog Star. It can be seen in both hemispheres, especially in January and February.

The Dog Star? Scooby-dooby-doo!

Yeah, that's your star, Scooby! It marks the chest of Canis Major.

CANIS MAJOR

Sirius

Sirius is made up of a bright star and another smaller fainter white dwarf star. It is 8.6 light-years from Earth.

The star that is close to Sirius in brightness is called Canopus. It is also called the South's Great Star. That's because it can be seen best from the southern parts of the world. Canopus is part of the constellation Carina.

FACT

Scientist Henrietta Leavitt came up with a way to measure how far stars were away from Earth. Her work allowed scientists to measure the distance of stars farther away from Earth than before.

Polaris is also called the North Star. It's important because of where it is in the sky. For hundreds of years, sailors have used this star to help them find their way. This star shows where north is because it sits above the North Pole.

You can find the North Star only if you are in the Northern Hemisphere. Find the Big Dipper. Draw a line between the two stars at the end of the scoop. They will point right to Polaris. The star is the tip of the Little Dipper's handle in the Ursa Minor constellation.

FACT

The star closest to our sun is the red dwarf Proxima Centauri. It's 4.25 light-years away. It would take us 80,000 years to travel there.

Polaris is the only star in the night sky that appears to remain still.

Rike a statue?

Not quite. It actually does move in a little circle around the exact North Pole each day!

Betelgeuse is the largest star that can be seen from around the world, except in Antarctica.

Bee-what? Did you say beetle juice? Like as in the bug?

YUCK!

Yes, but that's just the way you pronounce the star's name!

Betelgeuse is a red supergiant star. It's about 764 times the size of our sun, but it's not as hot. It's the second brightest star in the constellation Orion. It makes up the hunter's shoulder in this constellation.

It is especially easy to see between December and March. Betelgeuse is the 10th brightest star in our sky. It is about 640 light-years away from Earth.

Astronomers have noticed that Betelgeuse's brightness is changing. It's sometimes bright and sometimes dim. They think this means the star is coming to the end of its life.

When Betelgeuse finally explodes, scientists think it could shine as bright as the moon. We'd even be able to see it in the daytime. The death of this star could leave behind a black hole.

Stars of Orion

Orion is a constellation that can be seen from almost everywhere on Earth. The hunter's belt is most easily found because of the three stars that form a straight line. It has not only the bright star Betelgeuse, but also Rigel. This bright supergiant star is at the hunter's front foot. It's around 75 times the size of our sun and twice as hot.

Chapter 3

Pictures in the Sky

The International Astronomical Union (IAU) is a group of scientists that study the stars and the universe. They recognize 88 constellations today. Thirty-six of these are in the northern sky, and 52 are in the south.

The largest constellation, Hydra, is best seen in the southern sky. Hydra represents a sea snake in Greek mythology. The largest constellation in the north is Ursa Major, or the Great Bear.

HYDRA

Hydra covers more than three percent of the night sky.

A giant sea snake? I'm glad it's up in the sky, not down here!

Remember, it's just named after a story, silly!

CANCER

The constellation Cancer is the dimmest of all constellations. You can only see it if the sky is very dark. Looking at it from the Northern Hemisphere, the stars in this constellation make an upside-down Y. In the south, it's right side up.

Constellations and Mythology

Many constellations were named a long time ago by the Greeks and Romans. There are many Greek and Roman myths about the constellations. Cancer is a crab in Greek mythology. The story says the goddess Hera sent the crab to distract Heracles when he was fighting a monster. Heracles kicked the crab into the sky, and it now stays there.

Greek astronomer Ptolemy named the Cassiopeia constellation. It was named for a queen in Greek mythology. Queen Cassiopeia was placed in the sky along with her husband Cepheus and daughter Andromeda as punishment by the god Poseidon. Cassiopeia had been caught bragging about how beautiful her daughter was, and this displeased the gods.

Today, the three constellations of Cassiopeia, Cepheus, and Andromeda can be found side by side. Looking at the northern sky, Cassiopeia is recognized by the five bright stars that form a W shape.

CASSIOPEIA

Ptolemy also named Gemini. Astronomers have found eight stars in Gemini that have their own planets orbiting them. Gemini is also home to the Jellyfish Nebula. It is a **remnant** of a giant supernova.

A planet named Thestias orbits the star Pollux in Gemini. Scientists think it's a gas giant. These planets are large and made up of mostly gases.

Like, that planet must burp a lot!

Hee-hee!

It takes Thestias 590 days to orbit Pollux one time.

Chapter 4

Stars Help Find Our Way

Earth moves in the same orbit around the sun from year to year. The constellations are mostly in the same place each month.

In ancient times, people used the position of the constellations to tell them what time of year it was. They knew when to plant crops and when to harvest them based on the stars.

Ancient people also used the constellations to guide them across the oceans. If they found Polaris, they could figure out which way to go.

Today, scientists use the constellations as a sky map. They can use the positions of constellations to help them find areas of the sky they want to study.

Some maps show the 12 zodiac constellations. The sun appears to travel through these constellations during the year. They're used in astrology.

Hey! I've heard of those! They have signs for birthdays. Scooby's birthday is September 13, so he's a Virgo!

Reah!

FACT

Astronomer Margaret Geller made maps of the nearby universe. They have helped scientists understand patterns in galaxies. She has won many awards for her work.

Long ago, sailors used a tool called a sextant to help them find their way using constellations. A sextant measures the angle between the horizon and a star or other space object. This information can then be used to find a certain location on a chart.

Modern sextants help space travelers today.

In the 1960s, the U.S. space agency NASA sent some **astronauts** into space on the spacecraft Gemini. These astronauts used a sextant to measure their position in space. They used the position of the stars and constellations to guide them as they orbited Earth. This is called celestial navigation.

Today, spacecraft have computers that can do this job for astronauts. Still, on the International Space Station (ISS), astronauts practice using sextants. This can help them in case of an emergency.

Stars are groovy! I didn't know they were so important. I'll never look at them the same way again!

They sure are! And there's still so much to learn about them! Scientists continue to study stars in our galaxy and beyond.

Glossary

astronaut (AS-truh-nawt)—a person who is trained to live and work in space

astronomer (uh-STRAH-nuh-muhr)—a scientist who studies stars, planets, and other objects in space

atom (AT-uhm)—an element in its smallest form

element (E-luh-muhnt)—a basic substance in chemistry that cannot be split into simpler substances

galaxy (GAL-uhk-see)—a large group of stars and planets

gravity (GRAV-uh-tee)—a force that pulls objects together

hemisphere (HEM-uhss-fihr)—one half of Earth; the equator divides Earth into northern and southern hemispheres

kelvin (kel-VUN)—the base unit of temperature in the International System of Units

mass (MASS)—the amount of material in an object

nuclear fusion (NOO-klee-ur FYOO-zhuhn)—a process in which the nuclei of atoms are joined

planet (PLAN-it)—a large object that moves around a star; Earth is a planet

remnant (REM-nuhnt)—a piece or part of something that is left over

supernova (SU-pur-no-vuh)—explosion of a very large star at the end of its life that gives off tremendous amounts of energy

Read More

Hulick, Kathryn. *The Night Sky*. Abdo Books: Minneapolis, 2022.

Johnson, Kelsey. *Constellations for Kids: An Easy Guide to Discovering the Stars*. Rockridge Press: Emeryville, CA, 2020.

Lowery, Mike. *Everything Awesome About Space and Other Galactic Facts!* Orchard Books: New York, 2021.

Nargi, Lela. *Mysteries of the Constellations*. North Mankato, MN: Capstone, 2021.

Internet Sites

Ducksters: Astronomy for Kids: Constellations
ducksters.com/science/physics/constellations.php

Kiddle: Constellation Facts for Kids
kids.kiddle.co/Constellation

NASA Science Space Place
spaceplace.nasa.gov/menu/space/

Index

About the Author

Ailynn Collins has written many books for children. Science and space are among her favorite subjects. She has an MFA in writing for Children and Young Adults from Hamline University and has spent many years as a teacher. She lives outside Seattle with her family and five dogs.